Animals in the Wild

Kangaroo

by Vincent Serventy

ISBN 0-590-40226-9

Text copyright © 1983 by Vincent Serventy.
Illustrations copyright © 1983 by Vincent Serventy.
All rights reserved. This edition published by
Scholastic Inc., 730 Broadway, New York, NY 10003,
by arrangement with John Ferguson PTY. LTD.

12 11 10 9 8 7 6 5 4 3 2 1   12   6 7 8 9/8 0 1/9

Printed in the U.S.A.   24

SCHOLASTIC INC.
New York   Toronto   London   Auckland   Sydney

Most kangaroos live in Australia. There are about 50 kinds of animals in the kangaroo family. The biggest are the red kangaroos, and the eastern and western gray kangaroos. Here are some eastern gray kangaroos grazing in the bush.

Small and medium-sized kangaroos are known as wallabies. The ones in this picture are called pretty-face wallabies. When they are resting, they sit on their long tails.

Some kinds of kangaroos are very small. This one belongs to a
group called pademelon wallabies. When explorers from Holland
saw these kangaroos 300 years ago, they thought they were giant rats.

Some kangaroos are all white. Such animals are called albinos. These albino red-necked wallabies are grazing in an open-air zoo.

Red kangaroos live on the huge grassy plains of Australia. An old male "big red" may stand more than 6 feet in height and weigh about 150 pounds. A big kangaroo can defeat most enemies, even a wild dog.

This is a pretty-face wallaby on the move. Sometimes it is
called a whiptail because of its very long tail. When a
kangaroo hops, its tail does not touch the ground and its
body is balanced over its back legs.

A hopping kangaroo can reach a speed of about 35 miles per hour. If an enemy appears, a kangaroo can change direction easily, as this one is doing. An animal hopping on two legs uses less energy than one running on four.

Kangaroos are good jumpers. They can leap fences more than three feet high. Long jumps of over 12 feet are common; if in danger they can jump even farther.

Most kangaroos are good swimmers. Sometimes they hop into water to escape from danger. Here, a swamp wallaby stands in a pool glaring at an enemy. Kangaroos can swim across rivers and lakes.

Kangaroos are very friendly animals. They rarely fight, but sometimes they argue. Here, two male wallabies are wrestling. When they are wrestling, kangaroos use their tails to balance themselves.

Some kangaroos, like this yellow-footed rock wallaby, live in rocky hills. They hide during the day and come out to feed in the late afternoon and evening.

Some kangaroos live in trees. Tree kangaroos are found in the rainforests of north-eastern Australia. They eat leaves and berries. They jump from branch to branch or climb to the ground and hop to another tree.

All kangaroo mothers have a pouch to carry their babies.
It is a kind of bag. Inside are milk teats so the tiny
baby can feed. A baby kangaroo is called a joey. Here,
a joey stares out from the safety of its mother's pouch.

When baby kangaroos are born, they are blind and about an inch long. Yet they are able to climb up to their mother's pouch. They stay inside until they are big enough to look out at the world, as these twins are doing. Kangaroo twins are very rare.

This red-necked wallaby has a big baby in her pouch. A joey
will sometimes nibble at the grass or even hop out of the
pouch on a warm day.

A gray kangaroo joey lives for about seven months in the pouch before it looks out for the first time. By eight months it will spend a few hours every day hopping outside. At ten months it leaves the pouch for good.

Here, a joey is drinking its mother's milk. It will do this until it is about 18 months old. These are called red kangaroos. But the females are usually a bluish-gray, like the mother in this picture.

Big birds of prey, like this wedgetail eagle, can kill a young
kangaroo. But big kangaroos have few enemies, though they do
have to watch out for wild dogs, known as dingoes.

Acknowledgements are due to Vincent Serventy
for all photographs in this book except the following:
Hans & Judy Beste p. 13, 16; Ralph & Daphne Keller p. 11;
Trevor Pescott p. 9, 12; Dave Watts p. 18.